DAN FOX

The First Book of Chords
for Guitar

With additional information on Chord Progressions, Tuning,
Playing by Ear, Bass Notes, Transposition, Keys,
and
the Capo and how to use it.

Cover Photograph: David Attie

Photographic Illustrations: William Gerbracht

G. SCHIRMER, Inc.

DISTRIBUTED BY

HAL•LEONARD®
CORPORATION
7777 W. BLUEMOUND RD. P.O. BOX 13819 MILWAUKEE, WI 53213

T0051125

THE GUITAR
with Parts Named

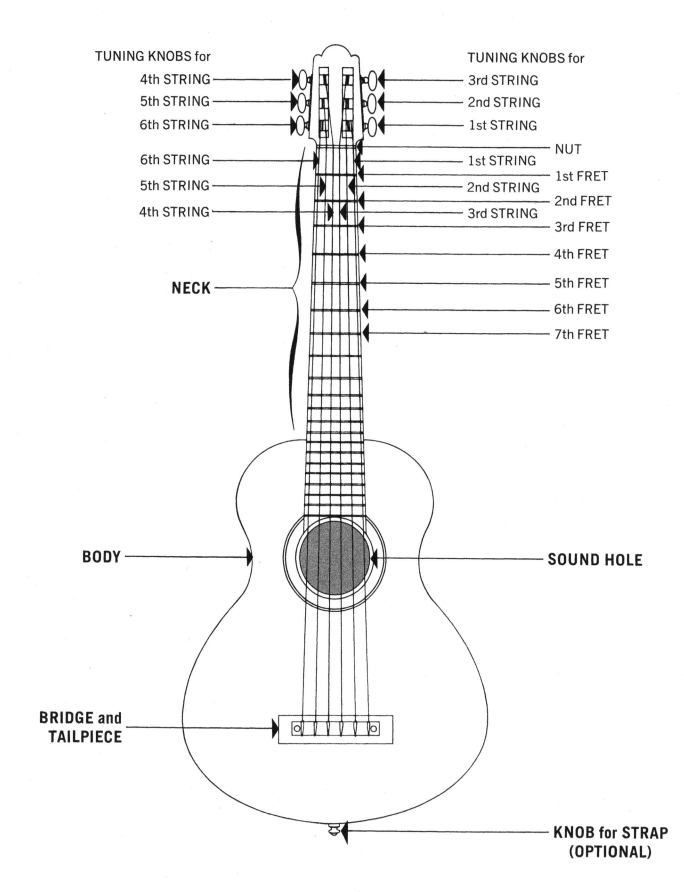

TUNING KNOBS for

4th STRING

5th STRING

6th STRING

6th STRING

5th STRING

4th STRING

NECK

BODY

BRIDGE and
TAILPIECE

TUNING KNOBS for

3rd STRING

2nd STRING

1st STRING

NUT

1st STRING

1st FRET

2nd STRING

2nd FRET

3rd STRING

3rd FRET

4th FRET

5th FRET

6th FRET

7th FRET

SOUND HOLE

KNOB for STRAP
(OPTIONAL)

FOUR DIFFERENT TYPES OF GUITARS

Classical Guitar **Folk Guitar** **f Hole or Jazz Guitar with electric pick-up** **Solid Body Guitar**

Any of the guitars pictured above can be used to play the material in this book. They are, however, designed for different purposes.

The Classical Guitar has a wide neck and is played finger-style (without a flat pick or finger picks). It is used to play classical music or relatively soft folk ballads.

The Folk Guitar has steel strings and is used to play folk, country and blues music. It may have a narrow neck or a wide neck.

The f Hole or Jazz Guitar specializes in jazz rhythm playing. With an electric pick-up mounted on it, it may be used for solo guitar too. The Hollow Body Guitar has f holes, but is essentially an electric guitar with some sound coming through the holes.

The Solid Body Guitar is totally electric. The hollow body and solid body guitar must be played through an amplifier. They are used for rock, amplified country music, soul and by some jazz players.

Although nylon string guitars are easier to finger in the left hand, their necks are wider and will cause you problems if you have small hands. They sound better for ballads and are essential for classical music.

Steel string guitars are good for folk, blues, country, rock and jazz. If you're using picks of any kind, you should have steel strings on your guitar.

If you do not already own a guitar we suggest that you rent or buy a steel string folk style guitar. This will avoid your having to buy an amplifier for the time being. As you progress further on the instrument you will want to concentrate on one or more styles of playing. At that point you should be careful to purchase the guitar best suited to the music of your choice.

FOUR WAYS TO HOLD THE GUITAR

1. Classical position with foot-stool

2. Seated with left leg over right

3. Seated with right leg over left

4. Standing with strap

STRUMMING CHORDS

Usually, chords are strummed with a downward motion of the thumb or hand.

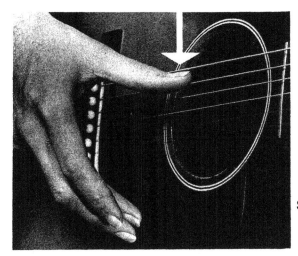

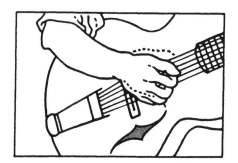

Strumming with the Open Hand

Strumming with the Thumb

Be sure to strum only the strings indicated in the diagrams.

STRUMMING WITH A FLAT PICK

Types of Flat Picks

Holding the Pick

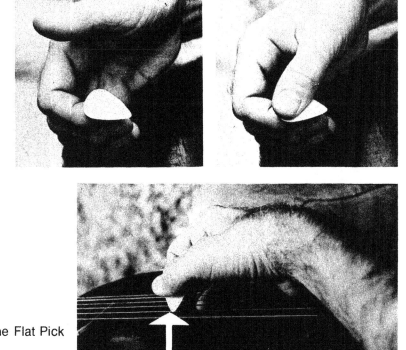

Strumming with the Flat Pick

When should I use a flat pick?

The flat pick is used for all rock songs, most blues and country songs, and any folk songs of a fast, rhythmic type for example, ("This Train"). More quiet folk songs, calypso, and pop songs are usually played without using picks. However, the sound you make is largely a matter of taste. Also, a flat pick will help you produce a louder sound if you're playing at a party or for group singing.

Consult the New Age Guitar Books by Dan Fox and Dick Weissman for more advanced types of strumming and finger-picking.

TUNING THE GUITAR

The best way to learn to tune a guitar is by watching and listening to a skilled player do it.

The next best way is to match the sound of each string with the recorded sound of a properly tuned guitar. There are many good tuning records available.

If neither of the above options is available, you may

Tune the guitar relatively, that is, without using any outside source. First, tune the 6th (lowest) string high enough so that it doesn't rattle or buzz against the fingerboard when struck. Then consult the diagrams below.

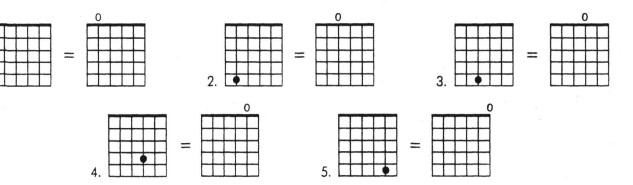

Here is what the diagrams show:
1. 6th string 5th fret is the same as the 5th string open.
2. 5th string 5th fret is the same as the 4th string open.
3. 4th string 5th fret is the same as the 3rd string open.
4. 3rd string **4th** fret is the same as the 2nd string open.
5. 2nd string 5th fret is the same as the 1st string open.

Tune to a piano:

The notes on the piano are:

On guitar they are written an octave higher in the treble clef:

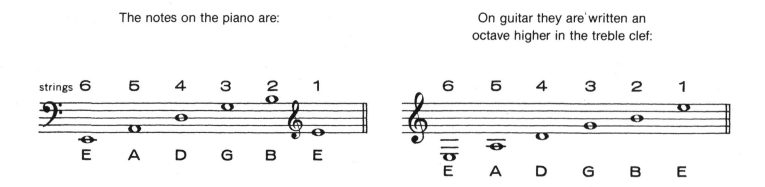

Last, and least recommended, is tuning to a pitch pipe. If a guitar pitch pipe is used, match the sound of each string with the appropriate reed sound of the pipe. If a chromatic pitch pipe is used, you must select the proper guitar notes, E, A, D, G, B and E.

HOW TO INTERPRET THE PHOTOGRAPHS, DIAGRAMS AND TABLATURE

On the following pages you will find all the basic chords used in folk, country, blues, rock and some pop and jazz. Each chord is explained in four ways:

1. A photograph shows the position of the left hand as it plays the chord. The photograph shows the hand position as viewed by the player.

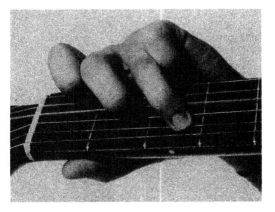

2. A diagram represents the six strings of the guitar. Circled numbers show you which fingers to use; zeros are open strings (strings not touched by the left hand); x's are strings not strummed.

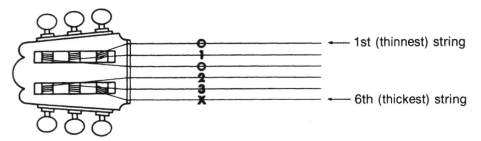

6th (thickest) string ⟶   ⟵ 1st (thinnest) string

3. Tablature is used to show the fingering on each string. The six lines of the tablature represent the six strings of the guitar. The numbers stand for frets (not fingers). O's mean open strings (strings not touched by the left hand); x's are strings not strummed.

⟵ 1st (thinnest) string

⟵ 6th (thickest) string

4. For those who can read it, I have included traditional music notation. However, keep in mind that guitar notes are written an octave higher than they actually sound, so that the C chord, for example, is written like Ex. 4a, but actually sounds like Ex. 4b.

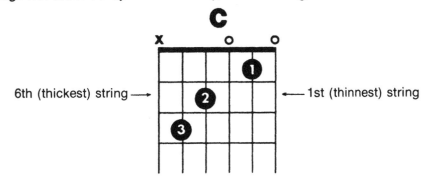

4a. Guitar notes   4b. Actual sound of 4a.

Note: The chords in this book are arranged by Chord Families. This is fully explained on page 28.

THE KEY OF **G** MAJOR (EASY VERSION)

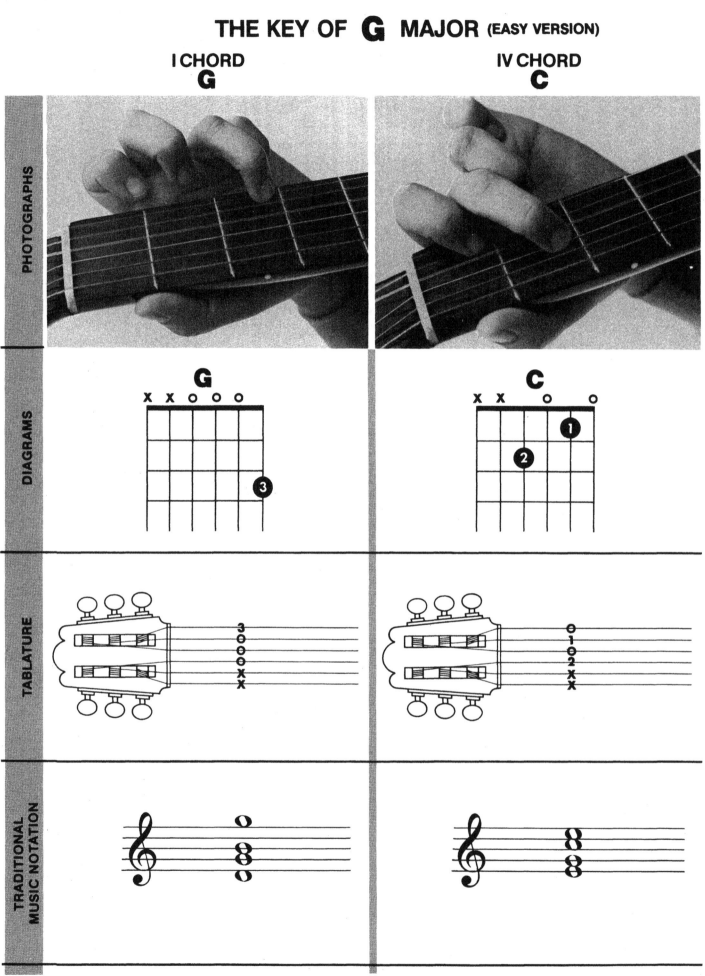

I CHORD
G

IV CHORD
C

PHOTOGRAPHS

DIAGRAMS

TABLATURE

TRADITIONAL MUSIC NOTATION

THE KEY OF **G** MAJOR (EASY VERSION)

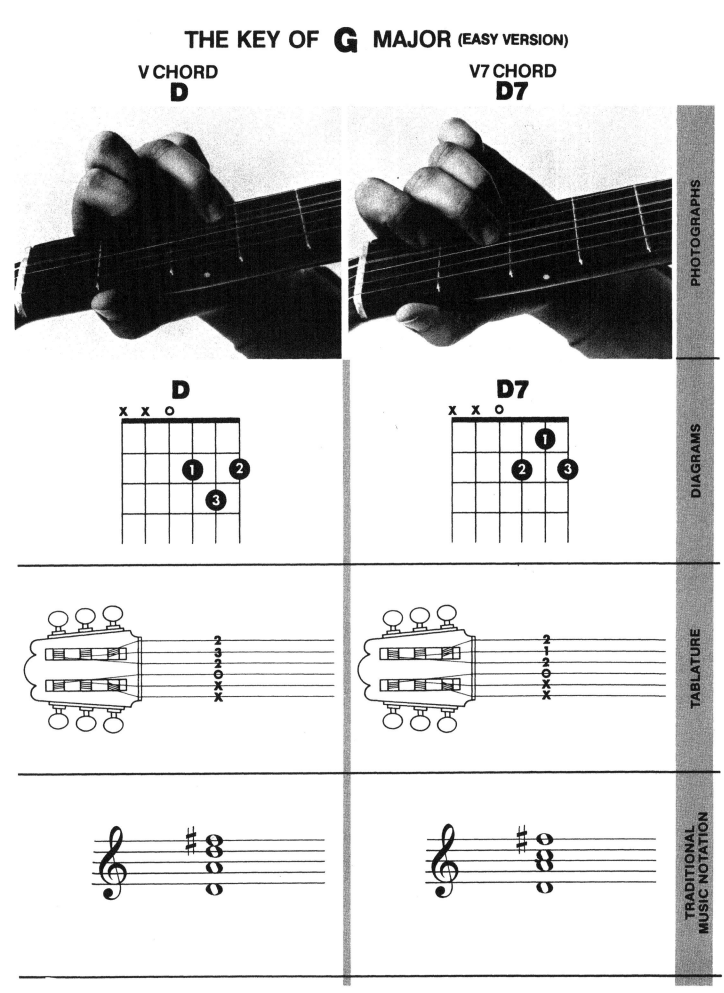

THE KEY OF **D** MAJOR

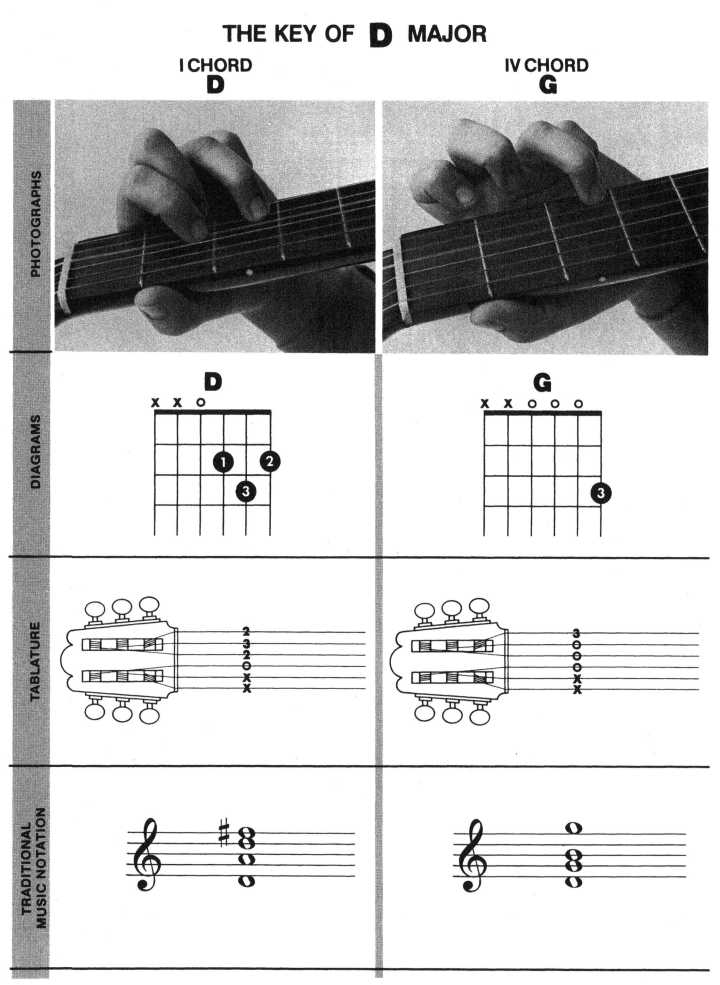

THE KEY OF **D** MAJOR

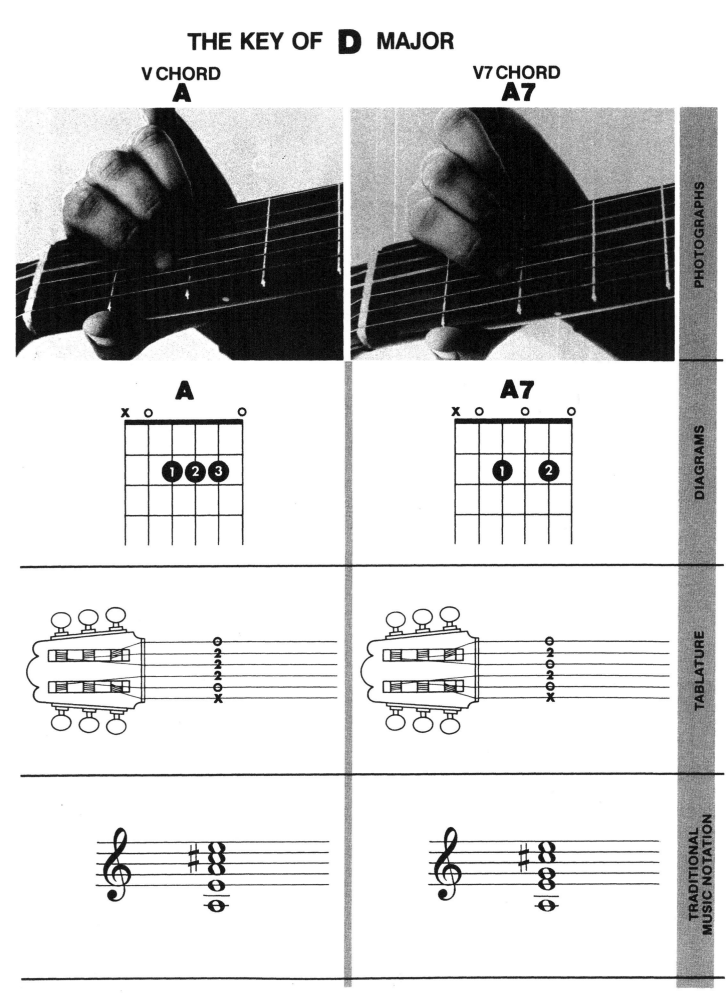

V CHORD
A

V7 CHORD
A7

PHOTOGRAPHS

DIAGRAMS

TABLATURE

TRADITIONAL MUSIC NOTATION

THE KEY OF **A** MAJOR

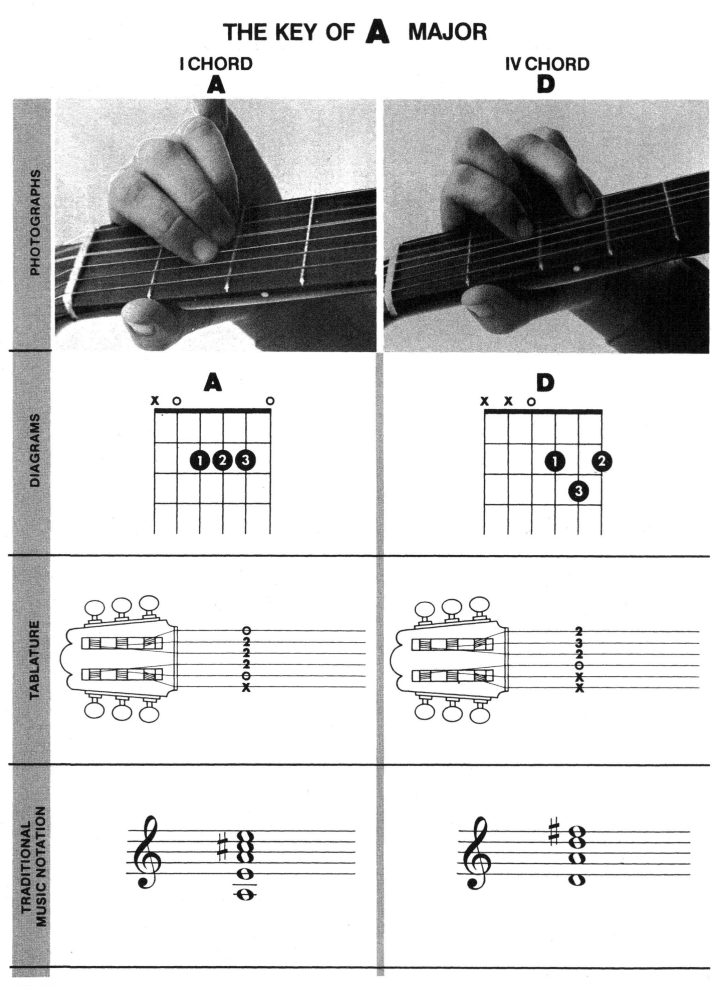

THE KEY OF **A** MAJOR

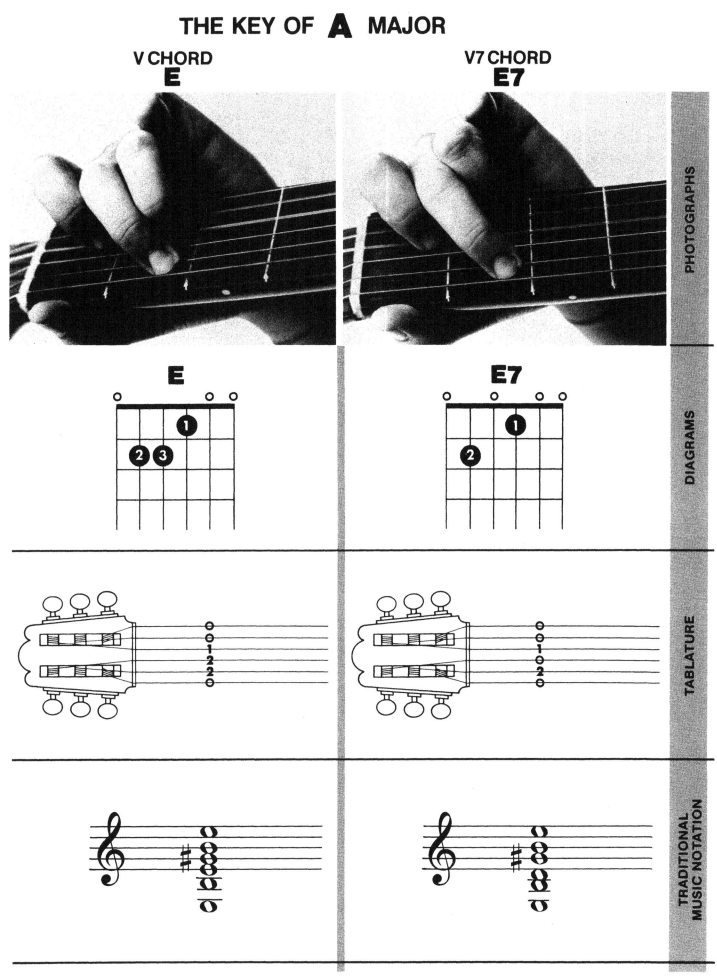

THE KEY OF **E** MAJOR

I CHORD
E

IV CHORD
A

PHOTOGRAPHS

DIAGRAMS

TABLATURE

TRADITIONAL MUSIC NOTATION

THE KEY OF **E** MAJOR

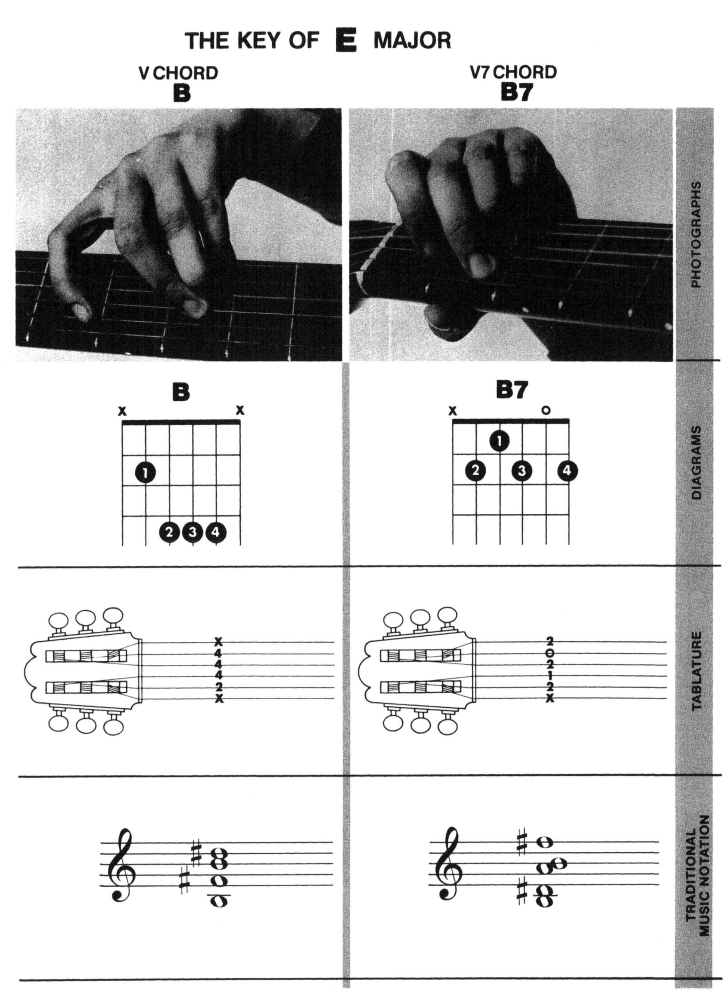

THE KEY OF **E** MINOR

THE KEY OF **E** MINOR

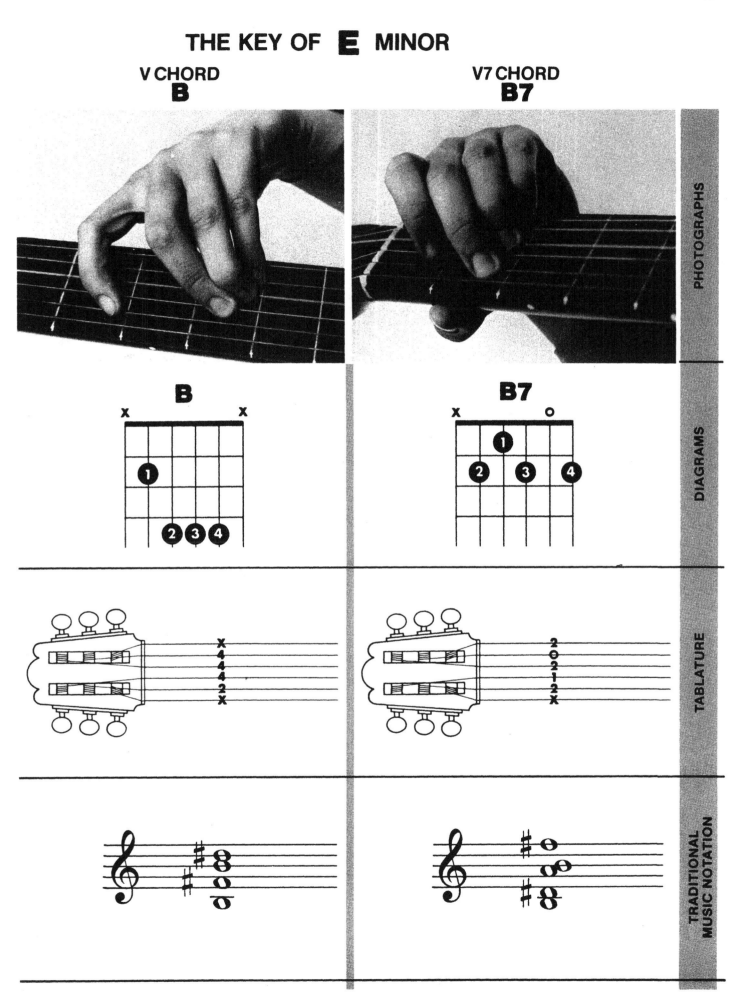

V CHORD
B

V7 CHORD
B7

PHOTOGRAPHS

DIAGRAMS

TABLATURE

TRADITIONAL MUSIC NOTATION

THE KEY OF **A** MINOR

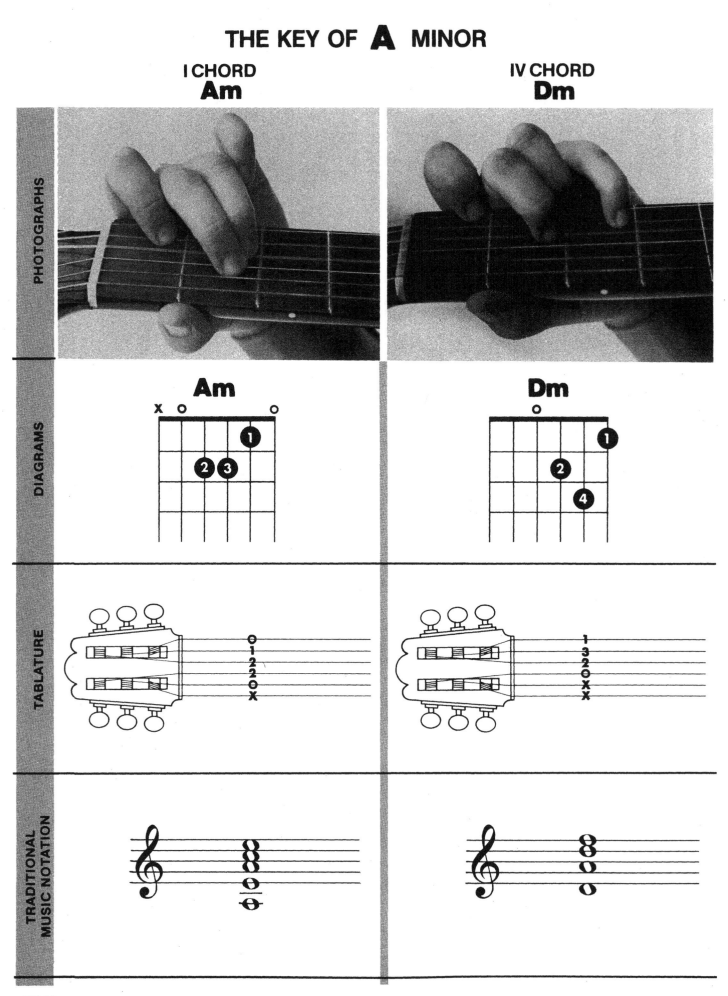

THE KEY OF **A** MINOR

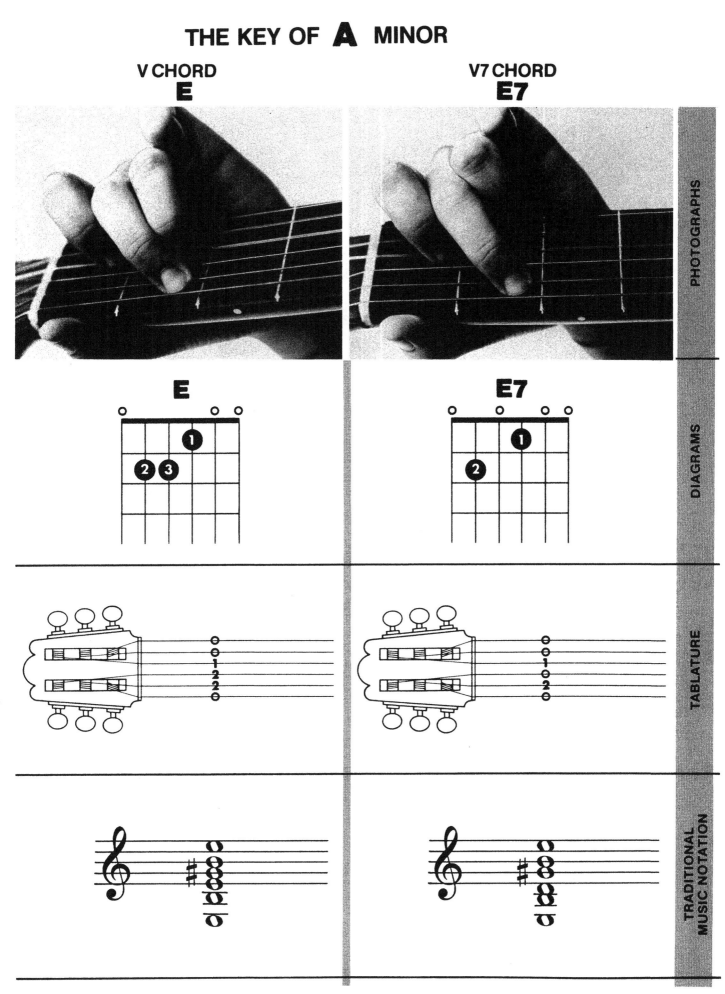

THE KEY OF **D** MINOR

THE KEY OF **D** MINOR

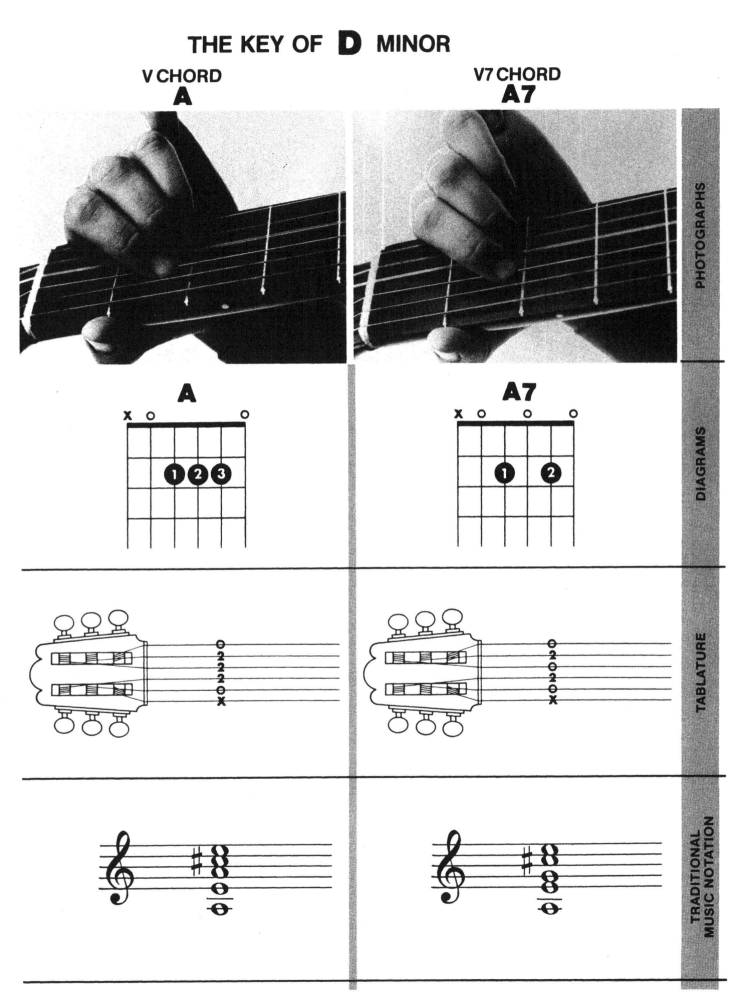

THE KEY OF **G** MAJOR (COMPLETE VERSION)

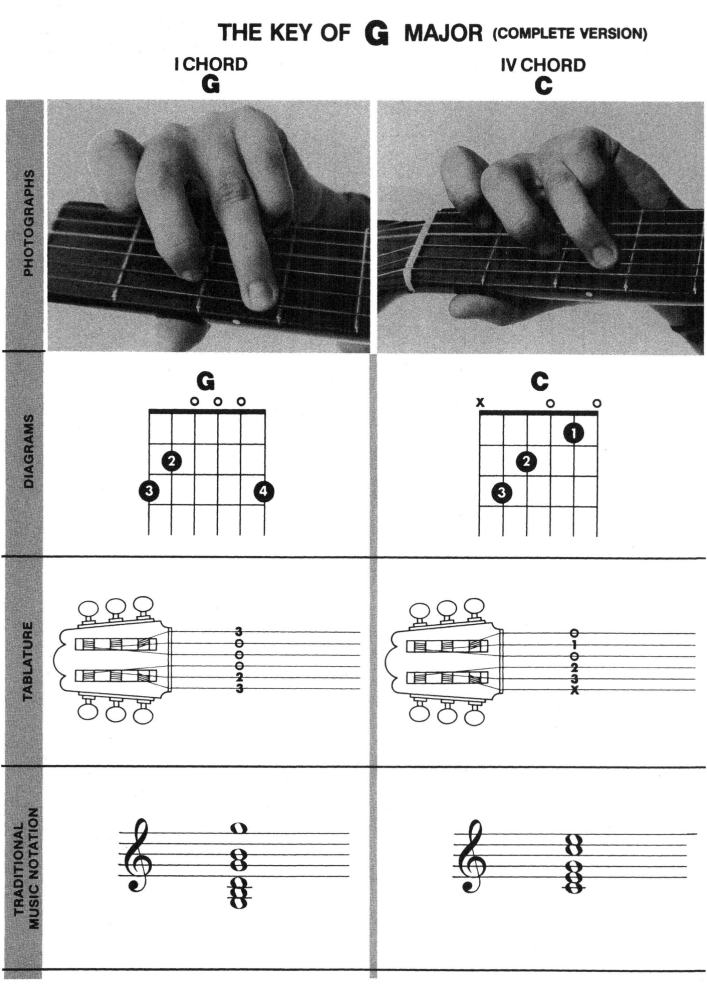

THE KEY OF **G** MAJOR (COMPLETE VERSION)

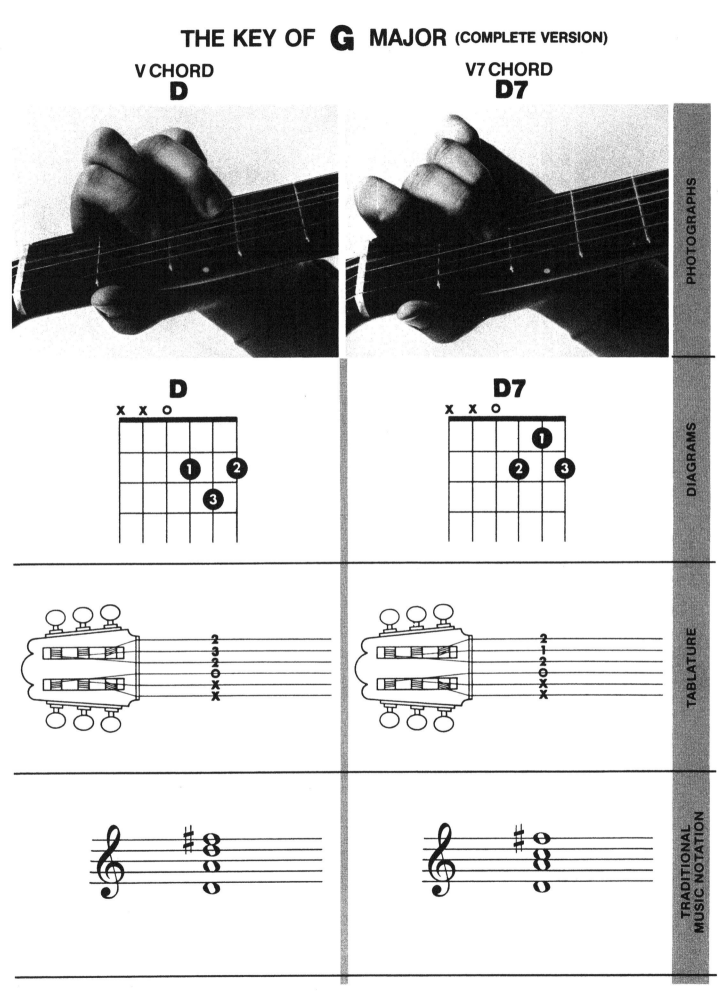

THE KEY OF **C** MAJOR

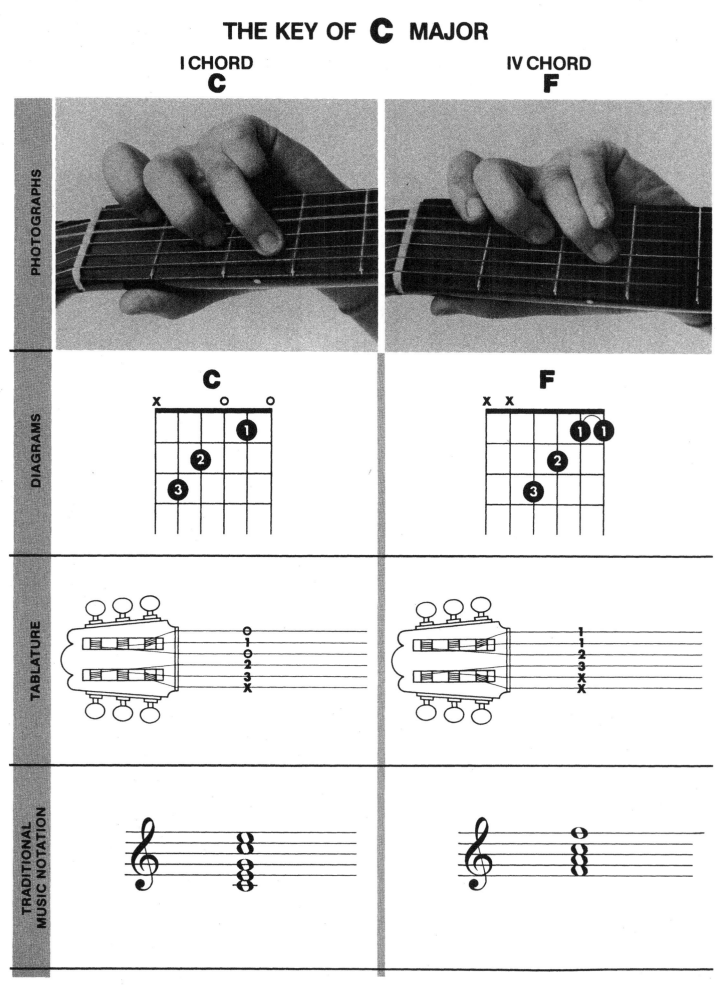

THE KEY OF **C** MAJOR

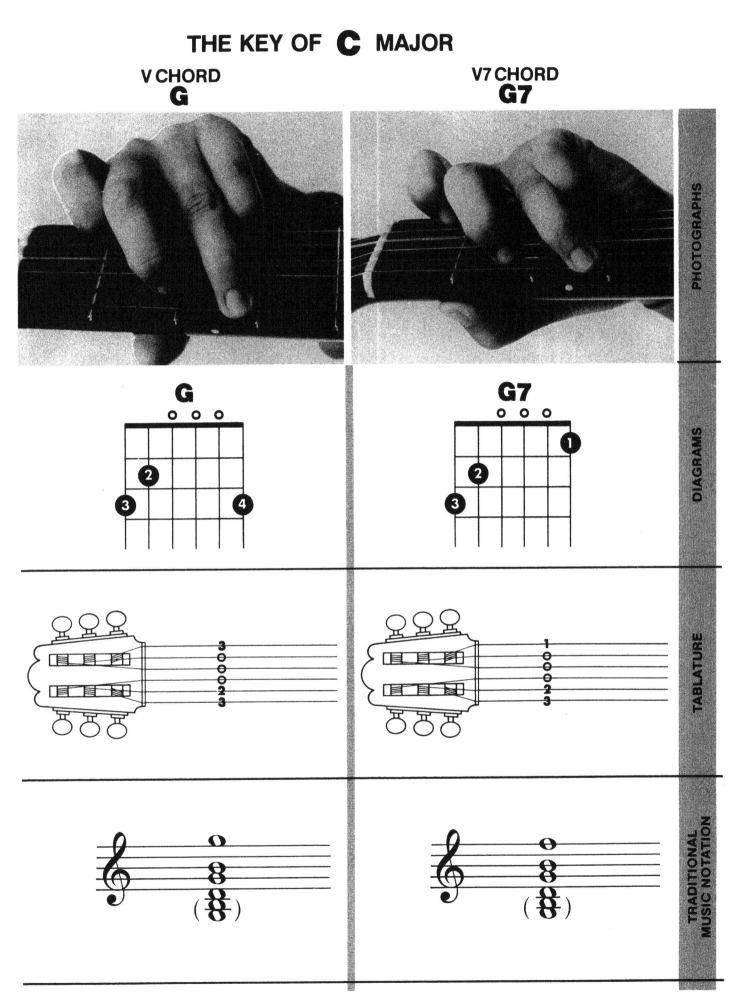

THE KEY OF B MINOR

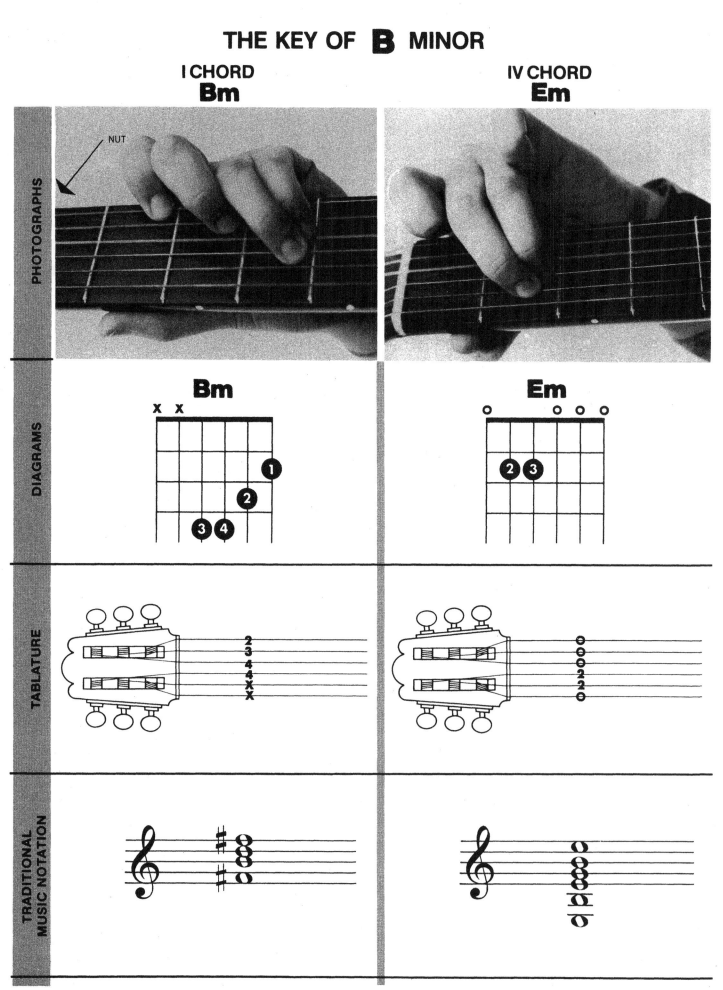

THE KEY OF **B** MINOR

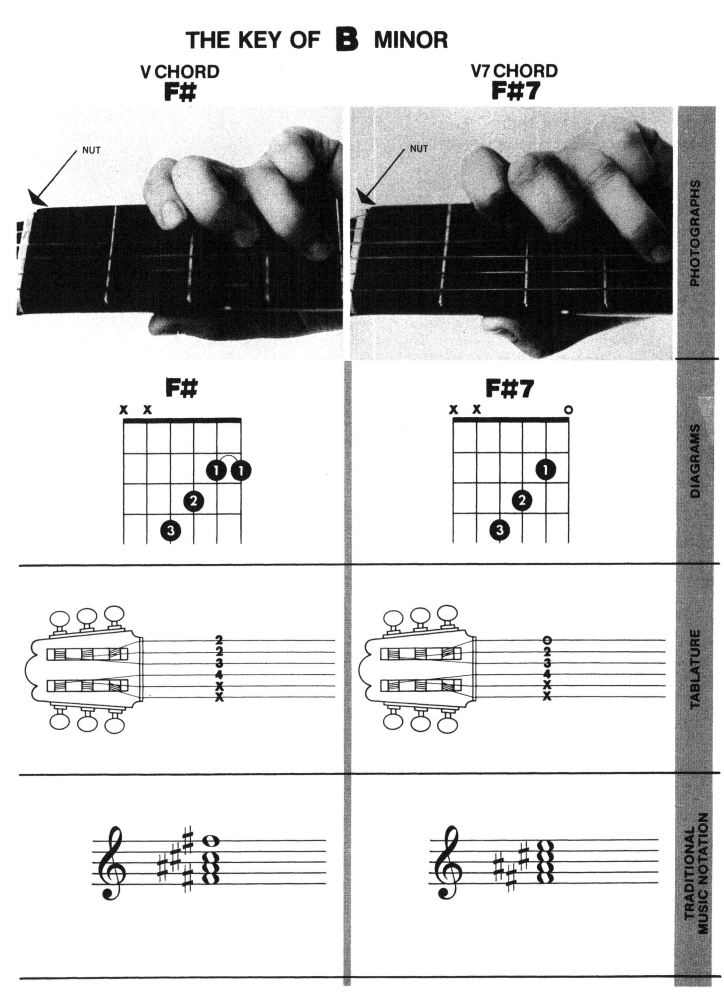

QUESTIONS AND ANSWERS ABOUT KEYS AND CHORD FAMILIES

On pages 8-27 you have seen chord families in all the commonly used "open string" keys.

Question: What is a chord family?

Answer: A group of closely related chords that often occur together in a song.

Q: What is a key?

A: A place from which a song begins and to which it eventually returns. Practically speaking, this means that the last chord of the song has the same name as the key in which the song is written. For example, a song in the key of C ends on a C chord, a song in the key of G ends on a G chord, a song in the key of D minor ends on a D minor chord. (This rule for determining the key works about 99% of the time. In very rare instances a song does not end on the key chord, but this is usually to give a deliberately unfinished effect. Listen to the Beatles' "And I Love Her" which is in the key of Eb but suddenly ends on a C major chord.)

Q: What do the Roman numbers stand for?

A: The Roman numbers refer to the chords in any key. The key chord is always I. Then, counting up the musical alphabet of A B C D E F G A etc., the IV and V chords are easy to find. For example, if I is A, then IV is D and V is E (I=A, II=B, III=C, IV=D, V=E). In the key of C, I=C, IV=F, V=G, etc. See the chart on page 29 for the I, IV and V chords in all possible keys.

Q: Are there such things as II, III, VI and VII chords?

A: Yes. They are used in some rock and country music as well as in most pop and jazz.

For more information on the above consult the Fox/Weissman New Age Guitar Book, Theory and Technique, published by G. Schirmer, Inc.

MAJOR CHORD FAMILIES IN ALL POSSIBLE KEYS
(Keys used in this book in bold face type)

Key	I	IV	V	V7
C	**C**	**F**	**G**	**G7**
C♯	C♯	F♯	G♯	G♯7
D	**D**	**G**	**A**	**A7**
E♭	E♭	A♭	B♭	B♭7
E	**E**	**A**	**B**	**B7**
F	F	B♭	C	C7
F♯	F♯	B	C♯	C♯7
G	**G**	**C**	**D**	**D7**
A♭	A♭	D♭	E♭	E♭7
A	**A**	**D**	**E**	**E7**
B♭	B♭	E♭	F	F7
B	B	E	F♯	F♯7
C♭	C♭	F♭	G♭	G♭7

MINOR CHORD FAMILIES IN ALL POSSIBLE KEYS
(Keys used in this book are in bold face type)

Key	I	IV	V	V7
A minor	**Am**	**Dm**	**E**	**E7**
B♭ minor	B♭m	E♭m	F	F7
B minor	**Bm**	**Em**	**F♯**	**F♯7**
C minor	Cm	Fm	G	G7
C♯ minor	C♯m	F♯m	G♯	G♯7
D minor	**Dm**	**Gm**	**A**	**A7**
E♭ minor	E♭m	A♭m	B♭	B♭7
E minor	**Em**	**Am**	**B**	**B7**
F minor	Fm	B♭m	C	C7
F♯ minor	F♯m	Bm	C♯	C♯7
G minor	Gm	Cm	D	D7
G♯ minor	G♯m	C♯m	D♯	D♯7
A♭ minor	A♭m	D♭m	E♭	E♭7

USING CHORD FAMILIES TO ACCOMPANY SINGING

After deciding on a song, pick any key that's easy for you to play in and strum the I chord. Start singing. Is this key comfortable for your voice? If it is, fine. If not, try different keys until you find one that works for you. Everyone's voice is different, so there is no definite rule for choosing a key. Also, women tend to sing four or five keys higher than men.

Question: How can I find out what key I sing in?

Answer: This question reflects a commonly held misconception. No one sings every song in the same key. Each song is different. If you sing "When The Saints Go Marching In" in the key of E, you'll probably sing "Yankee Doodle" in G. But there is a great deal of variation. For one thing, if you have even a halfway decent voice, you'll be able to sing any song in quite a few keys. If you have pretty high notes, you'll want to choose a key that's high enough to show them off. If you have power in the lower register, you'll choose a suitable key for that.

In addition, your voice will vary according to the time of day (most people sing lower earlier in the day), how tired you are, and whether you're sitting or standing (many people sing three or four keys higher when standing than they do when sitting down). Even the place you're performing in affects the key. You may want to sing in a higher key when performing in public; the extra effort you make in public will push your voice up a few keys.

One of the main advantages of knowing and using chord families is that it allows you to switch keys with little difficulty.

Once you've found a comfortable key, open this book to the appropriate page and go to it!

SONGS THAT USE ONLY TWO CHORDS

Some simple songs require only the I and V7 (or V) chords. Below are some examples: (/ means to repeat the same chord. That is, C /// means to play the C chord four times, once for the letter name and once for each of the / marks.)

CLEMENTINE

(I) I / / / / / / / / V7 /
In a cav-ern, in a can-yon, ex-ca-va-ting for a mine,

V7 / / / I / / V7 / / I /
Lived a min-er, for-ty nin-er, and his daugh-ter, Clem-en-tine.

I / / / / / / / / V7 /
Oh, my dar-ling, oh, my dar-ling, oh my dar-ling, Clem-en-tine,

V7 / / / I / / V7 / / I
You are gone but not for-got-ten, dread-ful sor-ry, Clem-en-tine.

CAMPTOWN RACES (1st part only)

I / / / / / // V7 /// / /// /
Camp-town lad-ies sing this song, doo - dah, doo - dah,

I / / / / / // V7 / / I //
Camp-town race-track's five miles long, Oh, doo - dah - day.

Note: Underlined words and syllables get a slight accent.

FRERE JACQUES

```
I  V7 I    /    / V7 I   /   /  V7  I/   /  V7  I /
Fre-re Jac-ques, Fre-re Jac-ques, Dor-mez-vous? Dor-mez-vous?
I      V7    I /   /     V7    I  /  /  V7 I/  /  V7  I
Son-nez les Ma-ti-nes, Son-nez les ma-ti-nes, Din-don-din, Din-don-din.
```

ROW, ROW, ROW YOUR BOAT

```
I    /    /     /     /      /      /      /
Row, row, row your boat, gent-ly down the stream,
I     /     /      /     V7   /     I    /
Mer-ri-ly, mer-ri-ly, mer-ri-ly, mer-ri-ly, Life is but a dream.
```

OH, SUSANNA (1st part only)

```
     I   /  / /  /  /  /  / /  / V7 / /
Oh, I come from Al-a-bam-a with a ban-jo on my knee,
 /    I   /  /  /  /  /  /  / /  / V7 I  I  / /
And I'm goin' to Lou-si-an-na  my Su-san-na for to see.
I  /  /  /      /  / /  /  /  /  / V7 / /
It rained all day the night I left, the weather it was dry,
 /  I  / / /  /  /  /  /  /  / V7  /  I  / /
The sun so hot I froze my-self, Su-san-na, don't you cry.
```

Here's a song in minor key that uses only two chords:

JOSHUA FIT THE BATTLE

```
Im     /    /    / / / / V7 / / / Im / / /
Josh-ua fit the bat-tle of Jer-i-cho, Jer-i-cho, Jer-i-cho,
Im     /    /    / / / /  /     V7   /   /   / Im / /
Josh-ua fit the bat-tle of Jer-i-cho and the walls came tumb-ling down.
Im    /     /      /    /  / / /
You may talk a-bout your kings of Gid-e-on,
 /      /     /      /    / / / /
You may talk a-bout the King of Saul,
 /     /    /   /   /  /  /  / / /   V7   /  / / Im
But there's none like good old Josh-u-a at the bat-tle of Jer-i-cho,
 /   /  /
That morn-in' (Repeat first two lines)
```

SONGS THAT USE COMPLETE CHORD FAMILIES

The majority of American folksongs and blues can be played using the complete family of the I, IV and V7 (or V) chords. This even includes many recently composed tunes by such writers as Paul Simon, Bob Dylan, John Denver, Chuck Berry and Elvis Presley. (See page 38 for a partial list of titles.) On the next two pages you'll find the chord progressions for several well-known folksongs and blues. Try to play them in as many keys as possible.

CARELESS LOVE

```
I / / /   V7   /   /   / I / / / / / / /
Love, oh, love, oh, care-less love,        _
I / / /   /   /   /   /  V7 / / / / / / /
Love, oh, love, oh care-less love,        _
I / / /  / / / /  IV / / / / / /
Love, oh, love, oh care-less love,
  /  I / /  /  V7  /  /  / I / / /  / / /
Just see   what love has done to me.        _
```

WHEN THE SAINTS GO MARCHING IN

```
        I  /  / / / /  /   /   / / / / /  /
Oh, when the saints     go march-ing in,        _
  /   /   / / / I r / / / / V7 / / /  / /
Oh, when the saints go march-ing in,        _
  / / I / / / / / / / / /  IV / / / / /
Lord, I want to be in that num-ber   _
  /   / I / / / / / V7 / I / / /  /
When the saints go march-ing in.        _
```

CAMPTOWN RACES (2nd part)

```
I  /  /  / / / / / / IV / / / / I / / /
Goin' to run all night,     Goin' to run all day,
I  /   /   /   / / / / V7  /  / / I / /
Bet my mon-ey on a bob-tailed nag, Some-bod-y bet on the bay.
```

OH, SUSANNA (2nd part)

```
IV / / / / / / / i   / / / V7 / /
Oh, Su-san-na, oh, don't you cry for me,
  / I / / / / / / / / / / V7 / I / /
'Cause I come from Al - a - bam - a with a ban-jo on my knee.
```

SILENT NIGHT

I / / / / / / / / / / / V7 / / / / / I / / / /
Si -lent night, Ho - ly night, All is calm, All is bright.

IV / / / / / I / / / /
Round yon Vir-gin Moth-er and Child,

IV / / / / I / / / / /
Ho - ly In - fant so ten - der and mild

V7 / / / / / I / / / / / / / / V7 / / I / / /
Sleep in heav -en - ly peace, ___ Sleep in heav - en - ly peace. __

AULD LANG SYNE

I / / / V / / I / / / IV / /
Should auld ac-quaint-ance be for-got And nev-er brought to mind?

/ I / / / V / / / IV / / V7 I / /
Should auld ac-quaint-ance be for-got, And days of auld lang syne?

IV I / / / V7 / / IV I / / / IV / /
And days of auld lang syne, my dear, And days of Auld Lang Syne,

/ I / / / V / / / IV / / V7 I / /
Should auld ac-quaint-ance be for-got, And days of Auld Lang Syne?

JOHN HENRY

I / / / / / / / / / / / /
When John Hen-ry was a lit-tle ba-by sit-tin' on his mam-my's knee,

/ / / / / IV / / /
He picked up a ham-mer and a piece of steel, said,

I / / IV I / IV / /
"This ham-mer'll be the death of me, Lord, Lord,

I / / IV I /
This ham-mer's gon-na be the death of me."

CHARLIE IS MY DARLIN'
(An old Scotch folk song in minor key)

Im / / / IVm / Im /
Char-lie is my dar-lin', my dar-lin', my dar-lin',

Im / / / / V7 I /
Char-lie is my dar-lin', the young chev-a-lier.

THE CAPO*

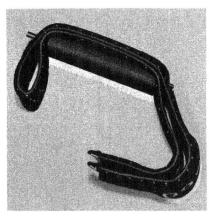

Capo in position at the 2nd fret
Notice that the capo is clamped straight
across the fretboard, directly behind—not on—
the fret.

Playing the D chord with the capo at the
2nd fret. The fingering of the chord remains
the same but it is played two frets higher
on the fretboard.

HOW THE CAPO WORKS

When the capo is in position, it shortens the effective length of each string by an equal amount. This means that the entire guitar will now sound higher than it did before. The higher the fret, the higher the sound. Practically speaking, this means that you can still play the same chords you already know, but they will sound in different, higher keys. This is of great value when a song is in too low a key for the singer. Just play the same chords but with a capo across the 1st, 2nd, 3rd, 4th, or 5th fret. I don't recommend placing it any higher than this because the strings become so short that they lose most of their tone and the guitar starts to sound like a ukulele. On the facing page is a chart showing the various keys you can play in using the same chords you already know with a capo across various frets.

*Most Americans say KAY-po, although the original pronunciation is KAH-po with the ah pronounced as in father.

TRANSPOSITION

Taking a song that is written in one key and playing it in a different key is called transposition.

TRANSPOSITION CHART

If you play in the key of	with a capo across the	You will sound in the key of
C	1st fret 2nd fret 3rd fret 4th fret 5th fret	C♯ or D♭ D E♭ E F
D	1st fret 2nd fret 3rd fret 4th fret 5th fret	E♭ E F F♯ or G♭ G
E	1st fret 2nd fret 3rd fret 4th fret 5th fret	F F♯ or G♭ G A♭ A
G	1st fret 2nd fret 3rd fret 4th fret 5th fret	A♭ A B♭ B C
A	1st fret 2nd fret 3rd fret 4th fret 5th fret	B♭ B C C♯ or D♭ D

The above chart can also be used for the keys of D minor, E minor, and A minor; just keep in mind that a minor key stays minor when the capo is in use. For example, if you play in the key of E minor with a capo across the 4th fret, you will sound in the key of A♭ minor. A chart for the key of B minor is below.

	with a capo across the	You will sound in the key of
B minor	1st fret 2nd fret 3rd fret 4th fret 5th fret	C minor C♯ minor D minor E♭ minor E minor

Notice that there is a lot of overlapping. For example, if you want to sound in the key of C, you can play in the key of C without a capo, play in the key of G with a capo across the 5th fret, or play in the key of A with a capo across the 3rd fret. Each of these three ways will sound in the key of C, but will have a different quality of tone. This can give a greater variety to your playing.

PLAYING BY EAR

Playing a song without music is called playing by ear. You must choose songs whose tunes (melodies) you know very well. The next step is to figure out the chords that go with the song. We'll start off with some simple songs that require only two chords, the I and V7 (or V, if you prefer).

Here's how to do it:

1. Select a key at random.
2. Open this book to that key and make sure you know how to play the I and the V7 chords.
3. Strum the I chord till you establish the mood, tempo (speed), and key of the song in your mind.
4. Keep strumming the I chord and start singing. If the key is comfortable for your voice, continue to step 5. If the key is too high or too low, start over in a different key.
5. Keep strumming and singing till the I chord doesn't sound right anymore. Then,
6. change to the V7 and keep strumming and singing till you hear the need of another chord.
7. Continue strumming and singing, changing back and forth between the I and V7 chords as you think necessary till the end of the verse or chorus. Keep in mind that the first and last chords will almost always be I, and that the next to last chord is V7.

Here's a practical example of the above:

SKIP TO MY LOU

1. Select a key at random. D major, for example.
2. Open this book to the key of D major, page 10-11, and make sure you can play the I chord (D) and the V7 chord (A7).
3. Strum the D chord at a moderate tempo. Try to hear the starting note of the song.
4. Keep strumming the D chord and start singing. If the key is comfortable for your voice, continue. Otherwise start over in the key of G.
5. Keep strumming the D chord as you sing "Fly in the buttermilk, shoo fly shoo." At this point your ear tells you that D will no longer sound good.
6. Change to the A7 chord and sing the next "Fly in the buttermilk, shoo fly, shoo."
7. Your ear tells you to go back to the I chord, D, and sing the third, "Fly in the buttermilk, shoo, fly, shoo."
8. Go back to A7 for the next to last chord and "Skip to my Lou my..."
9. Can you hear that the last chord has to be I? If you can, you now understand what a key is. It's almost like a "home base" that the song starts out from and eventually returns to. Sing the last "dar-ling" on the D chord.

SONGS TO PLAY BY EAR

Here's a list of mostly well-known songs that require only two chords to play, the I and V7. All are in a major key.

A-HUNTING WE WILL GO
ALOUETTE
BEER BARREL POLKA (1st two strains)
BILL BAILEY (1st half)
BILLY BOY
BLOW THE MAN DOWN
BUFFALO GALS
CAMPTOWN RACES (verse only)
CHOPSTICKS
CIELITO LINDO (verse only)
CLARINET POLKA (1st strain)
DID YOU EVER SEE A LASSIE?
DOWN IN THE VALLEY

DOWN ON THE FARM
GO TELL AUNT RHODY
GOODBYE, OLD PAINT
HAIL, HAIL, THE GANG'S ALL HERE
HE'S GOT THE WHOLE WORLD IN HIS HANDS
HINKY DINKY PARLEY-VOUS
LONDON BRIDGE
MARYLAND, MY MARYLAND
MEXICAN HAT DANCE
OH, CHRISTMAS TREE
OH, SUSANNA (verse only)
POLLY WOLLY DOODLE

MORE SONGS TO PLAY BY EAR

SANTA LUCIA (1st half)
SHALL WE GATHER AT THE RIVER (1st half)
SHOO FLY
SKIP TO MY LOU

TEN LITTLE INDIANS
TOM DOOLEY
WHERE, OH, WHERE, HAS MY LITTLE DOG GONE
THE YELLOW ROSE OF TEXAS

As mentioned before, the majority of American folksongs and blues as well as many other types of songs can be played using complete chord families of I, IV, and V7 (or V). The partial list below will give you some idea; your ear will suggest many more.

John Denver songs
ANNIE'S SONG
THANK GOD I'M A COUNTRY BOY
FLY AWAY
GRANDMA'S FEATHER BED (except for one chord in the bridge. Maybe you can find it.)
SUNSHINE ON MY SHOULDERS (1st half)
FOLLOW ME (Chorus only)
LEAVING ON A JET PLANE
FOR BABY (For Bobbie)

Paul Simon songs
I AM A ROCK
FEELIN' GROOVY (starts on IV)
CECILIA
BRIDGE OVER TROUBLED WATER (1st part)
ME AND JULIO DOWN BY THE SCHOOLYARD (1st part)

Woody Guthrie songs
THIS LAND IS YOUR LAND (starts on IV)
DEPORTEE
GOING DOWN THE ROAD
HARD TRAVELIN'
OKLAHOMA HILLS
ROLL ON, COLUMBIA
SO LONG, IT'S BEEN GOOD TO KNOW YUH, and most of the rest of his songs

Almost any traditional blues and talking blues or songs such as YOU AIN'T NOTHIN' BUT A HOUND DOG, BLUE SUEDE SHOES, THE TWIST, PEPPERMINT TWIST, AT THE HOP and hundreds of others that are based on blues. This also includes Chuck Berry's JOHNNY B. GOODE and MAYBELLINE, GUITAR BOOGIE and GUITAR BOOGIE SHUFFLE, the first and third strains of ST. LOUIS BLUES (the 2nd strain is in minor key), IN THE MOOD and many more.

The basic blues chord progression is

I/// I/// I/// I/// IV/// IV/// I/// I/// V/// IV/// I/// V///

This makes a total of twelve groups of four beats called bars or measures. After the last chorus, end on I instead of V.

MORE SONGS THAT USE I, IV and V7

BLOWIN' IN THE WIND
GOODNIGHT, IRENE
C.C. RIDER
WRECK OF THE JOHN B.
BABY, YOU'RE A RICH MAN

CAN'T BUY ME LOVE (verse only)
COME TOGETHER (minor I, major IV, and V)
GET BACK
GIVE PEACE A CHANCE
HEY, JUDE

BASS NOTES

After a while, strumming chords gets to be a little monotonous. Some of this monotony can be avoided by occasionally substituting a *bass note* for a chord.

A bass note (and by the way, bass is pronounced like 'base,' not like the name of the fish) is a low note, usually the lowest note in a chord. It is most often the same note as the name of the chord; the bass note for a C chord is the note C, the bass note for a D minor chord is the note D, etc. In more advanced playing you'll find that other bass notes can be used with each chord, but for now, stick with the ones given.

USING BASS NOTES

You may have noticed that all songs can be accompanied in groups of three (DOWN IN THE VALLEY, GOODNIGHT, IRENE, SO LONG, IT'S BEEN GOOD TO KNOW YUH) or groups of two (CARELESS LOVE, THIS LAND IS YOUR LAND, CAMPTOWN RACES, etc.)

When the song has rhythms in groups of three, you can substitute a bass note for the first chord in each group. Think "oom-pah-pah." Bass note goes on "oom," chords go on pah-pah. In music this is called three-quarter time, written 3/4. 6/8 time is simply two units of 3/4 one after the other.

Example:

I

Down	*in*	*the*	*val*	-	*ley,*			*Val-*	*ley*	*so*
bass note	chord	chord	bass note	chord	chord	bass note	chord	chord	bass note	chord	chord

V7

low			*hang*	*your*	*head*	*o*	-	*ver*		*etc*
bass note	chord	chord	bass note	chord	chord	bass note	chord	chord	bass note	chord	chord

In groups of two, think "boom-chick." Bass note goes on "boom," chord goes on "chick."

Example:

I   V7

Camp-	*town*	*lad-*	*ies*	*sing*	*this*	*song*	*Doo-*	*dah,*		*etc.*
bass note	chord	bass note	chord	bass note	chord	bass	chord	bass note	chord	bass note	chord

On the facing page there is a complete chart of all the chords used in this book with bass notes indicated.

CHORDS USED IN THIS BOOK

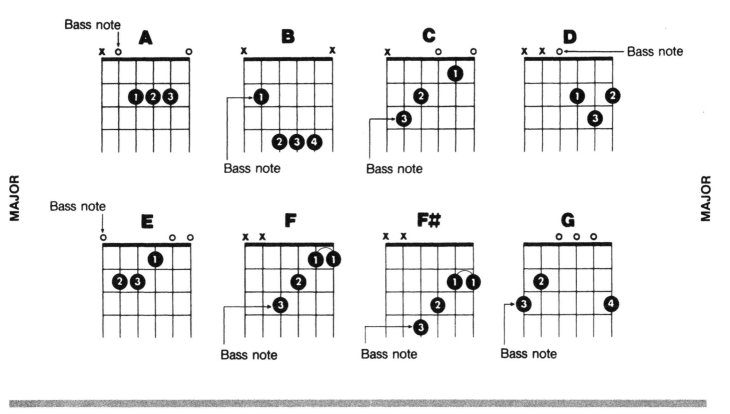

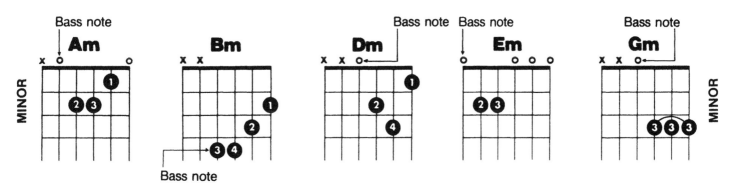

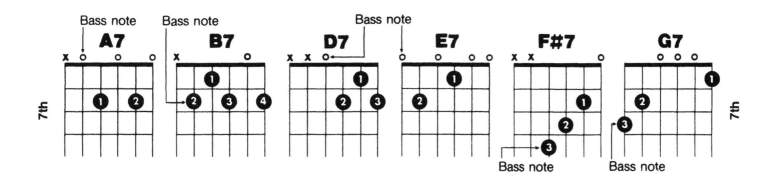

INDEX

WHERE TO FIND INDIVIDUAL CHORDS

These chords and thousands of others can be found in THE WHOLE BOOK OF GUITAR CHORDS by Dan Fox, and published by G. Schirmer, Inc., 866 Third Avenue, New York, N.Y. 10022.